Teesdale in Pictures
A photographic study

David Shaw

HAYLOFT

First published 2008

Hayloft Publishing Ltd, South Stainmore, Kirkby Stephen, Cumbria, CA17 4DJ

tel: + 44 (0) 17683) 42300
e-mail: books@hayloft.eu
web: www.hayloft.eu

ISBN 1 904524 59 1

A catalogue record for this book is available from the British Library

Printed and bound in the EU

Papers used by Hayloft are natural, recyclable products made from wood grown in sustainable forests.
The manufacturing processes conform to the environmental regulations of the country of origin.

To my dear wife, Angela, for her love, tolerance and support.

A bright autumn day in Birkdale - were the sheep pleased to see me or was the camera bag mistaken for a feed sack?

CONTENTS

Each season brings its own delights. The fresh, vibrant vitality of spring meadow land replaces the sombre black and white landscape of winter and in turn yields to the purple vista of August heather and autumn hues bring the 'back end' of the year to a blazing climax.

The Tees at Leekworth.

INTRODUCTION

As a boy growing up in the industrial heartland of the north east of England in the 1950s, there were two highlights to the year. The first was Christmas and the second, the annual camping holiday at Leekworth Farm near Middleton-in-Teesdale. Preparations for camping began weeks in advance. First the letter from my father (stamped addressed envelope enclosed) to Tom Dent asking if we could camp in his field for a fortnight, followed by the ritual packing of the trunk. It wasn't a very big trunk, an heirloom left by my grandmother, I think, but it held a prodigious amount. It would be collected by British Railways and sent 'Passenger's Luggage in Advance' to Leekworth to await our arrival. Finally the long awaited day of departure would arrive and we would leave home laden like Sherpas to walk the mile and a half to South Hylton station to board the train.

We lived like tinkers - cooked on a wood fire, washed in the river and explored the dale in the only way we could - on foot.

I knew, even then, that this was the place I wanted to live, the community of which I wanted to be a part, but it was a long way, or so it seemed then, from a Sunderland housing estate. Career opportunities were taken and jobs engineered to find employment within striking distance of Teesdale and, in 1987, we moved from Durham to Lartington. My work as an engineer involved a considerable amount of world travel and holidays now are taken in much more exotic locations than Leekworth, but the magic of Teesdale throughout the seasons remains undiminished.

So what was the idea behind this book? Well, it was never meant to be a guide book, except from the comfort of an armchair; neither is it a learned tome on the history, geology and botany of the area, though all these subjects are touched on. It is simply and unashamedly a picture book which aims to celebrate the beauty and diversity of the Teesdale landscape by the only method I know, that is through the lens of a camera.

Regarding the photographs, most were captured digitally, and processed using a photographic software package. I should confess here to removing the odd electricity pole and television aerial but otherwise they are accurate records of the scenery as seen on the day. I hope that you will enjoy looking at them as much as I did taking them.

August at White Force.

THE SOURCE TO COW GREEN

Boundary stone and the source of the Tees.

"The river Tees rises on the south east shoulder of Cross Fell in Cumberland, the highest point in the Pennine range..." were the opening words of a guide book to upper Teesdale published in the 1960s. This little book provided inspiration to explore the valley by describing many popular walks in the area. However, it did not (so far as I can remember) include a photograph of the source of the Tees and, to tell the truth, I did not intend to do so either.

The plan was to go to Trout Beck Bridge, point a 300mm lens towards Cross Fell, and call the resulting photograph 'Tees Head'. To do so would have been accurate and saved considerable effort but it would have been a cop out; how could I start a book with an admission of failure? The only problem was getting there; Tees Head is a long way from anywhere. There is a road (the highest in the country) which leads from the village of Knock, in the Eden Valley, to the radar station on the top of Great Dun Fell.

I knew that the upper section of this road is private but had hoped to be able to drive as far as the access to Silver Band mine. This hope was dashed by a sign - 'End of public road no unauthorised vehicles' - not far outside Knock. Although I would rather drive than walk, being a law-abiding citizen, there was no option

The road to Great Dun Fell and the Radar station.

but to pick up the camera bag and walk. Fortunately, on this occasion I was accompanied by my wife who wanted to see the 'golf ball' at close quarters. How could I disappoint? Without this 'encouragement' I may have resorted to the original plan.

There is parking for a couple of cars near a gravel pit opposite Knock Pike at the beginning of the private road. From here, at an altitude of 300m the summit of Great Dun Fell, at 848m, is about four miles away. The road climbs steadily, following the steep-sided valley of Knock Ore Gill with its abandoned quarries and mining remains, towards poetically named Green Castle fell. About half a mile further on there is a choice of routes. The road can be followed, or alternatively, the Pennine Way branches off to the right across Dunfell Hush (more about hushes later) - either way leads to the summit of the fell.

Many unkind words have been spoken and written about the radar station operated by the National Air Traffic Service on Great Dun Fell. Admittedly it looks totally alien, almost like a space station, which, tired of orbiting, has decided to settle on this remote fell top. But it's a friendly looking pile, visible from many places in Teesdale and beyond.

The path skirts the perimeter fence, descends, and then climbs to the flat top of Little Dun Fell which, at 842m is only six metres inferior to its big brother. The descent to Crowdundle Head is mostly well paved but crosses some very boggy sections where care is required if wet feet are to be avoided. The rocky slopes of Cross Fell loom ahead, but watch out for a crossroads marked by a stone in the path, a short distance beyond the gate. This stone is inscribed P.W. (Pennine Way) ahead and behind, and inexplicably the Greek letter omega to right and left. The way to the source of the Tees is to the right, a gate in the electric fence a little lower down leads in a few yards to the boundary stone.

Cross Fell, formerly known as Fiends Fell, may appear to be a vast featureless hump but it boasts some impressive statistics. At 893m (2,930 feet) its summit is the highest point in the Pennine range and the most lofty mountain in England outside the Lake District. Just to reinforce its credentials, its boundaries enclose the greatest area of land over 2000 feet high in England. The fell is mostly composed of carboniferous limestone which surfaces in an almost continuous rim around the stony summit plateau. The thin soils, acidic peat and climatic conditions combine to provide a habitat suited to rare alpine plants including starry saxifrage and forget-me-not.

There are several routes to Cross Fell, the villages of Kirkland and Garrigill are convenient starting places or the route from Knock described on the previous

Great Dun Fell, Little Dun Fell and Cross Fell.

Looking down from Tees Head.

pages may be followed. Whichever way is chosen, the final section is on exposed inhospitable terrain, making clear weather essential; this is not the place to be in mist.

The name Fiends Fell may derive from the meteorological phenomenon known as the Helm wind, Cumbria's answer to the Mistral, and the only named wind in the country, which shrieks like a banshee down the steep scarp slope of the fell to dissipate itself in the Eden valley. Locals describe it as a lazy wind because it can't be bothered to blow around you and goes straight through instead. Legend has it that the demons were banished from the fell by St. Augustine who erected a cross and an altar on the summit. Well the fiends may have gone, but the Helm wind certainly hasn't.

Experts in matters topographical will recognise the landscape opposite as a prime example of MAMBA which stands for miles and miles of not a lot!

Four miles from its source the Tees scores a double first when it is joined by its first major tributary, Trout Beck, and crossed by its first bridge. The bridge carries a road from Garrigill to the original Moor House, now demolished, which was a shooting lodge for the Appleby estate. It is feasible to drive to Trout Beck foot from Garrigill, given a suitable vehicle (there are some serious potholes) and, with hindsight, this is probably an easier route to Dun Fell.

Trout Beck (left) joins the Tees and, below, Trout Beck bridge.

The road climbs out of Garrigill and follows the course of the river South Tyne, up to its source where a sculpture marks the place of its birth (if only the source of the Tees was so easily reached) and then descends to Trout Beck. The crumbling remains of buildings and spoil heaps bear testimony to the lead miners who toiled in this inhospitable place.

Even bright sunshine and a blue sky can do little to relieve the bleakness of this landscape. The Pennine Way traverses the Dun Fells and Cross Fell and there is the good track from Garrigill to Knock but between them is only coarse grass, peat hags and bog, I'm cer-

Waterfalls on Trout Beck.

tain that anyone with sufficient determination could walk from Tees Head to Trout Beck Bridge but would anyone choose to? Apologies here to botanists who will, no doubt, find the area with its unique plant life utterly fascinating.

There is not a path downstream from Trout Beck but exploration can be continued by following a track which leaves the Middleton to Alston road about a quarter of a mile south of Crookburn Bridge. This leads in time to Greenhurth mine which among the expected shafts and spoil heaps retains an almost intact wheel pit, the water wheel which powered the mine is alas long gone. The mine, which employed sixteen men below ground and eight above, was opened in

The view upstream from Trout Beck.

Greenhurth Mine.

1896 and closed in 1902. 1,654 tons of lead ore and 21 tons of zinc, with a total value of £11,918 were extracted in its lifetime.

Conspicuous in the view from Greenhurth are several blocks of isolated forestry. These were planted about forty years ago by the Forestry Commission as an experiment to determine the feasibility of afforestation in the locality, apparently they grew horizontally for the first ten years and the project was abandoned. The track continues from Greenhurth down towards

Cow Green reservoir

Fortunately it appears (to a layman) to have done little harm and the little gentian can be seen in May and June alongside the road from the car park to the dam.

Teesside industry has declined greatly over the last forty years and in that sense Cow Green is now redundant, however, it still fulfils an important role in river regulation. Without it water levels in drought conditions would fall drastically to the detriment of river life in general and migratory fish in particular. Immediately below the dam a bridge over the river carries the road and Pennine Way to the isolated valley of Birkdale and ultimately to High Cup Gill and Dufton.

Maize Beck which flows through Birkdale has a vast catchment area comprising Mickle Fell, Murton

the car park at Cow Green passing more mining remains on the way.

Cow Green reservoir was constructed between 1968 and 1971 to regulate the flow of the river for the benefit of Teesside industry. There was considerable controversy at the time because of fears that it would destroy the habitat of the unique flora of the area particularly that of the spring gentian which grows only here and on the west coast of Ireland in these climes.

Spring Gentian and Cow Green Dam.

Road to Birkdale.

Fell and Meldon Hill and is a major tributary of the Tees joining the river just below Cauldron Snout. Under spate conditions the flow down the beck can exceed (thanks to Cow Green) that of the river. Waterfalls close to Birkdale Farm, reputedly the highest farm in England, look interesting but unfortunately

Maize Beck, Birkdale.

no right of way exists to enable their exploration.

Make the most of the two trees at Birkdale farm - they're the last this side of Dufton! The path continues up the valley passing the ruins of Moss Shop mine. The red flag flying here does not mark the last outpost of the Russian empire, neither does it adorn an important summit but it does warn that you may be blown up by missiles from the army range over the hill at Warcop.

Mickle Fell from Moss Shop.

Confusion can arise at Moss Shop as the path appears to lead directly to the flag, in fact it continues along the crest of the spoil heap soon becoming a con-

spicuous track up the fell side.

Birkdale means "the valley of the birch trees" and although it must be many years since their demise, evidence of their former presence remains. There are peat hags here of mammoth proportions which preserve in their acidic depths sections of tree trunk with the silver bark still intact. As a rough guide, peat accumulates at approximately a foot (30cms) in 400 years, dating these trees to about 2000BC.

Presumably the wood, lacking its protective covering of peat, and exposed to the air will quickly deteriorate and rot away. However, this can't be the last of the Birkdale birches and further remnants will surely be uncovered as erosion by water and boots continue. It would be nice to see the slopes of the valley re-clothed in silver birch. Is there not some agency, per-

Peat hag and (above) preserved Silver Birch.

haps it could be Natural England, or something, that could take on the project?

The path continues across the slopes of Meldon Hill before descending to rejoin Maize Beck. The beck can usually be forded easily to gain access to High Cup Plain but in spate conditions it is safer to continue to the foot bridge, erected to prevent further fatalities after an accident some years ago.

I never intended to include High Cup Gill in this book, after all it can not claim any foot hold in Teesdale, precipitation falling into its depths is destined for the Eden rather than the Tees but after toiling up Birkdale some reward is deserved. High Cup Gill, often called High Cup Nick (the Nick is the narrow gap at the top) is a vast U shaped valley carved out by a glacier, at least that's the official version. I think it was gouged out by demons escaping from St. Augustine on Fiends Fell!

High Cup Gill.

High Cup Nick, Eastern crags and Western crags.

Looking back...

WIDDYBANK TO CAULDRON SNOUT

The walk from Widdybank farm or Moor House as we must now call it, is as varied as it is delightful. The walk to Moor House, if starting from the cattle grid on Peghorn Lane, is not. Special three cornered whin chippings guaranteed to be felt through any boot sole seem to have been selected to surface the road. Not too many years ago you could drive to Widdybank, park and get a pot of tea and a scone if you wanted. That was before it was taken over by English Nature, now Natural England. The landscape around Moor House has been deforested, grazed, mined and quarried, flooded and drained, so it is no longer in its 'natural' state.

The Tees flowing just outside Moor House has just emerged from an approximately 27 inch diameter pipe. It is, I think, another manifestation of the 'nanny state', everything must be classified, targets set and information boards erected. I confi-

dently expect to see 'No Smoking' and 'Keep off the Grass' signs here before too long. I'm sure that the people working at Moor House are pleasant, dedicated folk with the best of intentions. It's the people in city offices who assume that everything not actually covered in concrete is natural and unchanged since time began.

Well now that I've got that off my chest, where were we? Oh yes, bemoaning the state of the road to Moor House. Fortunately there is a much more pleas-

Cronkley and Widdybank.

Cronkley Scar and Cronkley bridge.

ant alternative though it does add another hour to the journey. Vehicles can be left at the Hanging Shaws picnic site just off the main road near Forest school. Fifty or so yards along the road in the direction of Langdon Beck, a track leads off to the left and passes farm buildings to arrive at Cronkley Bridge. The bridge is not crossed on this walk, instead the footpath to the right, marked Pennine Way, is followed upstream along the river bank. Views across the river are dominated by the crags and gullies of Cronkley Scar, perpetually it seems, in shadow.

Harwood Beck and Wheysike House.

The walking is delightfully easy, over soft grass at first, with the Tees providing musical accompaniment as it hurries along its stony course. The trout fishing here, by permit only, is very good; the fish though admittedly small - ten inches would be a good one - fight like little demons. It is not unusual when fishing with three wet flies on a cast, the traditional method in the area, to hook more than one fish at a time, the ensuing battle as the trout join forces to confuse the angler providing great sport. Such redoubtable opponents should (usually) be returned to fight another day, but, as an occasional treat a brace simply fried in butter makes a delicious breakfast.

After about a quarter of a mile the lush meadow is left behind, the path passes through a kissing gate and crosses a section of moraine and naked rock. At this point Harwood Beck joins the Tees. It would be possible (except in spate conditions) to ford the beck and continue along the river bank but no right of way exists here; instead follow the beck and cross at Saur Hill Bridge.

The Pennine Way continues straight ahead after crossing the bridge and skirts around Sayer Hill farm to traverse rough, rush covered, boggy terrain (bridges provide dry passage over the worst bits) and rejoins the river bank within sight of Widdybank Farm.

It has to be said that the view ahead does not inspire much enthusiasm for the task in hand. The landscape

Above, downstream from Saur Hill Bridge and below, the view upstream from Saur Hill Bridge.

is austere at best and seems to promise little of interest for some considerable distance. However, the walking is easy, either downhill or at worst flat, and Moor House is reached very quickly. From here the prospect improves no end. A good path, paved in places, follows the river first across a meadow and then along the base of the crags which gradually increase in height and ruggedness culminating in the whin sill bastion of Falcon Clints. I should say that I am aware that there are other starting points than Hanging Shaws, particularly near Langdon Beck Youth Hostel, but these necessitate roadside parking.

Widdybank.

The riverside path scrambles over piled up boulders, climbs the slopes and descends back to the riverside. In late summer scarlet bunches of rowan berries vie with the deep purple of the heather in a contest to provide the most colourful display. More secretively mountain pansies hide amongst the coarse grasses and harebells present their delicate blooms between the jumbled rocks along the way. It is said that peregrine falcons nest on the crags (hence the name Falcon Clints). I cannot claim to have ever seen them but one bird which can often be seen is the red grouse whose call of 'go back, go back, go back' should not be heeded, at least, not yet.

Rounding the bend in the river at Lingy Holme,

Looking back towards Cronkley, red grouse and harebell.

Maize Beck comes into view causing the hearts of those who have been expecting Cauldron Snout to be just around the next corner to descend rapidly into their boots. The beck occupies the place in the view, i.e. straight ahead, that has been the preserve of the Tees since leaving Widdybank. If it were the river then clearly the likelihood of there being a 200 foot waterfall within a reasonable distance is out of the question. Fortunately, it's a tease; one which becomes apparent as the last few hundred yards of the path beneath the crag is completed. Quite suddenly the corner is turned and Cauldron Snout comes into view.

Cauldron Snout is a series of cataracts - the Tees hurls itself over a descent of 200 feet in a distance of about 400 yards from its first leap from the sky line to the final roaring white fan of water at its base. Mind

An aerial view of the route and, above, Maize Beck.

Cauldron Snout.

you, the view point needs to be chosen carefully to avoid Cow Green dam being the sky line!

The 'path' links a series of heathery ledges to the right of the falls. It is awkward, involving some scrambling and high steps but not difficult or dangerous in normal conditions. However, in winter when the rocks are covered in ice, it's probably best left alone.

A circular walk is almost always more satisfying than one which retraces the route used on the approach. This circle can be completed by following the nature trail track up to the road and turning right along Peghorn Lane. There are some remains of the lead mining era along the way and the occasional glimpse into Harwood to enliven the journey but, in this case only, I prefer to go back the way I came.

Cascades and Cow Green reservoir from the nature trail.

HOLWICK AND CRONKLEY

Holwick Scar.

The hamlet of Holwick is over-shadowed by the near vertical cliffs of Holwick Scar, another out-crop of the ubiquitous whin sill. As a callow youth and keen rock climber with more testosterone than sense, I set out to explore the crags. We climbed several routes on the left side of the crag and decided to attempt an ascent of the middle section which I imaginatively named 'Central Buttress'. The starting point, as far as I can remember (it was 40 years ago), was close to the detached boulder just to the right of centre and went straight up to the tree which was a bit smaller then.

Rock climbs are usually divided into bite-sized pieces called pitches; this allows the leader to tie on to the crag, and the second man to climb part way up to join him. Protection in the form of running belays (rope or wire slings attached to the rock) is used at every opportunity. On this climb neither was possible. There was nowhere to stop and attempts to fix runners only resulted in them sliding back down the rope. The route started well enough but after about twenty feet the holds became smaller, covered in lichen and sloped downward. Adrenaline levels increased exponentially to the distance to the bottom of the crag. It was with a great sense of relief that I arrived at the tree and, heart pounding, tied myself to it. I may or may not be the first man to climb 'Central Buttress' but I bet I was the first in Teesdale to hug a tree! Climbing on the crags is controlled now and there are several no go areas - check on the web before you go.

At the end of the lane a path to the right of the house leads beguilingly between rocky outcrops and after passing Holwick Lodge joins an estate road over an area of rough grazing. The walking is easy being comparatively level and dry under foot with panoramic views of the north side of the valley. After about a mile the path, sign-posted Bridle Way leaves the road on the right and crosses boggy rush covered ground; sphagnum moss and peat predominate here but an easy way through can usually be found, stepping stones over the worst bits having been thoughtfully provided by previous travellers.

Evening at Holwick.

The next obstacle to be encountered is Blea Beck which rushes down from its source on the slopes of the intriguingly named Hagworm Hill, the watershed with Lunedale, to its fate at Bleabeck Force where it enters the Tees half a mile or so above High Force. Crossing the beck presents few problems in dry weather, the easiest passage being slightly upstream from the path. After heavy rain, however, care is required to avoid a soaking.

odically burnt to encourage regeneration and growth of new heather required by the birds for food, while other areas are left to provide shelter. This accounts for the

This is grouse shooting country, part of the world famous Holwick and Wemmergill territory. The red grouse cannot be reared in captivity (though someone is trying to in Scotland). Its success depends on the maintenance of its preferred habitat, namely heather moorland. To this end, sections of the moor are peri-

Clockwise from above, Blea Beck, a grouse butt and a busy day at the office.

patchwork appearance of a well-maintained grouse moor. Fortunately this management regime benefits many other species particularly waders such as curlews and oyster catchers.

After crossing Blea Beck the path climbs over two small rocky outcrops each crowned with a cairn; the heather clad slopes of Noon Hill are on the left and the wide vista ahead is dominated by the bulk of Cronkley Fell. The Green Trod, an old drovers road, is conspicuous in the scene as it rises to the summit of the fell.

Cronkley Fell from Dry Beck.

About half way into the previous photograph, the green trod is joined by a path, actually part of the Pennine Way, which leads over white ground to Cronkley Bridge. Over the bridge the track continues past Wat Garth to join the main road at Hanging Shaws picnic site. This is an alternative starting point to this walk, one which shortens the distance but misses the rock scenery of Holwick.

The green trod, steep in places, is followed between banks of heather and bracken to the summit of the fell.

Cronkley Scar from Hanging Shaws.

The views in retrospect are spectacular particularly in August and early September when the heather colour is at its best.

In contrast to the colourful approaches, the top of Cronkley is almost drab, but certainly not without interest. This is sugar limestone country and of major geological importance. Several large areas are fenced off to prevent erosion. How it survived for millennia without a wire fence to protect it is to be wondered at! The flat top of the fell affords views over Cow Green reservoir, seen as a thin blue line, to Great Dun Fell with its radio masts, Little Dun Fell and, in the distance Cross Fell, the highest point of the Pennine range.

The way across the flat summit is well cairned leading to the descent to the riverside below. It is here, in

Anti-clockwise from above: Noon Hill, from Cronkley Top, and Sugar Limestone and spring.

the opinion of your humble scribe, that the best view of the day is obtained.

In years gone by this route was used (by some) as an approach to Cauldron Snout necessitating fording

either the Tees or Maize Beck but that was in a far more robust era; wading across cold fast flowing water is probably not a good idea.

The path follows the river downstream through areas of boulders, bracken and bog (the worst bits are conveniently bridged) passing below the crags of Fox Earths, Raven Scar and Cronkley Scar. Unfortunately the rock scenery is not seen at its best due to an intervening shoulder of high ground. A better view is obtained from the other side of the river, an area we

Raven Crag

will visit later.

After about a mile, though it seems more, the path leaves the shadow of the crags and crosses rough pasture to arrive at Cronkley Bridge. If Hanging Shaws is the objective, cross the bridge and follow the track across the fields to the road. If returning to Holwick, turn right along the farm road and join the Pennine Way passing between High and Low crags, watch for a junction of paths near two standing stones and bear left. The way continues over thoughtfully provided foot bridges passing Dine Holm Scar (picturesque) and Force Garth quarry (less so) on the other side of the river to arrive at the charming waterfall of Bleabeck Force, this is the beck crossed earlier in the day.

High Force appears a little further on, its central rock, especially in summer, no doubt seething with

Dine Holm Scar and Bleabeck Force.

humanity in all shapes and sizes. Though the jewel in Teesdale's crown, High Force will not be described here. Waterfalls seldom look their best from above and this is no exception but, don't worry, lots of pictures later on!

After High Force, have a quick look from the viewpoint on the left of the track. A plantation of juniper is entered before arriving at Holwick Head House. Pass in front of the house then do a quick right and left, over a stile and on to the track leading to Hield House; the dogs are friendly and the cockerels colourful. The road can then be followed past Holwick Lodge, hidden in the trees, back to the starting point below Holwick Scars. This is an excellent expedition and full of interest but make no mistake, it's a long way. A pint in the Strathmore Arms may be called for and is certainly deserved.

Holwick Head House

MIDDLETON TO HIGH FORCE

When describing the course of a river it would seem logical to start at the top and work down. In the main, that is the approach I've taken in this book. However, for this section I decided to reverse the direction and work upstream. The reason for this is simple: the countryside between High Force and Middleton is charming whichever direction is taken but there is no doubt that the drama and excitement increase as the valley is followed upwards.

From the centre of the village walk down Bridge Street and cross the County Bridge. The riverside path, marked Pennine Way, starts on the right between the cattle market and the telephone exchange.

Middleton village green, above, and County Bridge.

45

The way begins through meadows which in spring provide a colourful carpet of wild flowers, and crosses many and varied examples of the stile builders' art to arrive high above the Tees, almost opposite the hamlet of Newbiggin. Here the view broadens; to the west are the high Pennines above High Force and beyond, while to the east is a more pastoral scene and the gentler prospect of the valley stretching back towards Middleton.

At this point the path descends to river level and continues through more meadows close to the settlement of Holwick. The grand house here is Holwick Lodge, part of the Strathmore estate and used by shooting parties on the world famous grouse moors of Holwick and Wemmergill. Closer to the river a camp

Left, the Pennine Way path, and above,
a spring meadow.

site and camping barn provide more humble accommodation for those more interested in walking the moor than shooting grouse flushed from it. Nevertheless, grouse shooting is a very important part of the Teesdale economy. The two major estates, Raby and Strathmore, provide employment and contribute to the environmental conservation of a vast area of high, heather moorland.

The path continues pleasantly enough slightly above river level to arrive at Scorberry bridge. It is now a much more elegant structure since the original tubular steel supports, which were regularly bent by floating tree trunks when the river was in spate, were encased in masonry in the late 1990s. Our route lies

Above, view upstream and, to the right, view downstream.

Meadows at Holwick.

not across the bridge - a footpath leads to Newbiggin that way - but continues alongside the river. Wainwright, in his *Pennine Way Companion*, considered the stretch of river between Scorberry and Winch Bridge to be the finest on the Tees; an accolade that would be accepted by many.

A riverside stile and Scorberry Bridge.

Above Scorberry Bridge

Between Scorberry and Winch bridges.

The next section of the walk is at its best either early or late in the year. The bluebells of spring and the blossom of early summer giving way to the rich reds and russets of autumn when the gold of the larches and crimson of rowan berries dominate the scene. Fungi too, both on the trees - beech in particular - and beneath them, add their own contribution to the extravaganza of seasonal colour.

A little further on the Tees flows in a deep gorge leading up to Winch Bridge. The present suspension bridge replaces an earlier structure built to convey lead miners from Holwick across the river. The original bridge collapsed, with some loss of life in 1802. An

Bluebells and May blossom.

Fly Agaric, fungi on beech and rowan berries.

information board close by tells the full story.

The name Tees is derived from the Norse word 'tess' (a reminder of the Viking invasions of the 9th and 10th centuries) which means boiling and refers to the appearance of the river at such places as Low Force where the water really does appear to boil. A famous view of the falls is to be had from the 'Yorkshire' side of Winch Bridge where a viewing point has been

Winch Bridge

thoughtfully provided.

There must be hundreds of thousands of photo-graphs of Low Force; I have quite a few myself! These pictures have been chosen to show how the scene changes depending on the height of the water and the

Evening at Low Force

light conditions.

The channel to the right of the main falls is dry when the river is at 'normal' height but after heavy rain becomes a series of cataracts. This is the preferred route for salmon which can often be seen at the back end of the year (September–October) negotiating the

river to reach their spawning grounds above.

Above Low Force the character of the scenery changes. The meadows of the lower reaches are replaced with rough grazing, trees become more sparse and the great whin sill with its columnar jointing becomes more apparent. The footpath, probably the most trodden in Teesdale, continues on the left bank (looking upstream) and after a short distance arrives at an island (or two depending on the water level) in the Tees. If the height of the water permits it's worthwhile

Winter and summer

crossing over to the (upper) island to see the river below another waterfall constrained to a narrow channel before entering a wide deep pool.

Continue the traverse of the island to rejoin the main path to Holwick Head Bridge. From here steps let into the hillside lead up to a gate then through a copse of juniper

Holwick Head.

affording views of the Tees in its gorge far below.

The objective of our journey is very close and, at least when the river is high, will be heard before it is seen. A path to the right leads through juniper to the

Summer spate, High Force

view point where the splendour of High Force is revealed as it thunders over the worn columns of the whin-sill.

The previous picture was taken in early summer, the photograph below is taken from the same place in winter.

Winter spate, High Force

Of course there is an easier way to see High Force, you can drive (and thousands do), park at the High Force hotel and saunter gently down a well surfaced path to view the falls from below.

High Force at mid-winter

HUDESHOPE

Hudeshope Beck enters the Tees just upstream of the County Bridge at Middleton, having completed its five mile course from its source high on the watershed between Weardale and Teesdale. The lower section of the valley, locally known as Beck Road, provides a pleasant Sunday afternoon stroll and a popular exercise route for dog walkers. Here the road

From left, Hudeshope and Kirk Carrion, Horseshoe Falls and wild rose.

follows the beck through a steep sided, wooded valley adorned with waterfalls and wild flowers; a truly idyllic setting. However, it was not ever thus. Fifty or so years ago this was the main rubbish tip for upper Teesdale!

The metalled road ends at a stone bridge spanning

Lower Bridge Beck road.

the beck close to a group of disused lime kilns. These were built to produce quick-lime from the stone won from Skears quarry above the kilns. The earliest kiln (second from the right) was constructed in the 18th century and renovated in 1939. Its neighbour, to the left, followed in the second half of the 19th century and that on the far left was built in the early 1900s. The kiln on the right (now totally collapsed) was constructed in 1941 to satisfy the wartime demand for lime. Production ended in 1960. An adjacent information board explains the process and dates each of the s t r u c t u r e s . Exploration of the valley can be continued from this point by choosing from three routes.

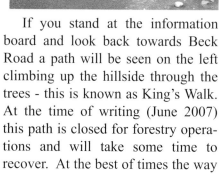

If you stand at the information board and look back towards Beck Road a path will be seen on the left climbing up the hillside through the trees - this is known as King's Walk. At the time of writing (June 2007) this path is closed for forestry operations and will take some time to recover. At the best of times the way

King's Walk and Upper Bridge

can be very muddy in parts, nevertheless it's a beautiful walk, particularly on a winter's morning when mist wreaths the landscape. There are good

kilns continues up the slope passing Skears quarry and leads through the wood, up a stairway cut into the hill side to arrive in open pastures. A little further on the beck is rejoined and the character of the valley changes dramatically. The gentle, sylvan beauty of Beck Road gives way to a much harsher landscape. Hudeshope beck now weaves its course between the spoil heaps and ruined buildings of the long abandoned lead mining industry which flourished here and in many other areas of the Pennines until its demise in the 19th cen-

views of the upper valley towards Aukside which reveal something of the area's lead mining history and roe deer and squirrels (alas only greys now) can often be seen. The path ultimately rejoins Beck Road near its junction with the Middleton to Stanhope road.

The second route from the lime

Lime kilns and Low Skears.

tury. As the road is approached the scene is dominated by the Coldberry mine complex, with its adits, shafts and mine shop clustered beneath the spectacular scar of Coldberry Hush etched into the hill Mining here ceased in the 1930s but I remember the spoil heaps being worked in the mid 50s, perhaps for the extraction

Coldberry

of fluorspar which would have been considered waste by the miners.

To take the third route from the lime kilns, follow the road over the bridge. Ignore the paths which go through the gate and bear right past the barrier over the track. The way continues passing an old tip reclaimed by nature, which now supports a colourful array of flora and provides a generous crop of wild raspberries in season, between stands of spruce and larch, to arrive at a watercourse issuing from a mine entrance on the left. At this point the path climbs the hillside above the mine but it's worth continuing ahead a little way to visit the limestone gorge of Jack Scar where Hudeshope beck, constrained by vertical cliffs, emerges from the dark interior. The path continues up through a plantation of conifers to arrive in open pastures above and to the left of Jack Scar. From here gated stiles in the dry stone walls lead eventually to the road on the Aukside side of the valley.

Either route taken from the lime kilns will arrive at

Jack Scar and Upper Hudeshope.

the road which encircles the valley. In the case of the first route, this will be to the east of Coldberry, while the second route will join the road at Club Gill, just to the south of the mine where a track to the left, just after the gate, across the road, leads to the mine buildings. The way from the first route is obvious.

Coldberry is not pretty. The word that springs to mind is devastation, nevertheless it is interesting and worthy of exploration. The main entrance to the mine is directly behind the mine 'shop' where miners lived during the working week. Further down the track, well away from the other buildings, is the powder house used for storing explo-

Coldberry Mine, left, and the wheel pit, above right

sives. The whole area surrounding the mine is covered in spoil heaps which even now support little vegetation. Behind the mine shop, at a higher level, are the remains of a water wheel pit used to supply power for the mine. Evidence of aqueducts used to lead water to drive the wheel can still be seen contouring across the fellside.

Above, the upper mine and below, looking north; right, Coldberry Gutter.

Exploration of the fellside above the mine buildings reveals more workings, ruined buildings, spoil heaps, shafts (approach with caution), and adits are encountered before reaching the great gash of Coldberry Hush. Hushing was a form of open cast working. Water was stored in reservoirs, the dams of which were breached to produce a tremendous rush of water which removed the over burden to expose the mineral veins. Evidence of hushing can be seen in many parts of the dale but Coldberry gutter is probably the most spectacular.

Red Grooves Hush

ing. We continued until we came to stone that had originally been part of the roof lying on the floor. At this point the instinct of self preservation took over and we returned to the daylight.

At Pikestone the path forks. To the left is a track leading down to ford the beck. This may be easy or impossible, depending on the height of the water, and from there to another area of mine workings at Newberry Scar. The entrance to these mines is guarded by steel gates, giving a perfect excuse (if one were needed) to stay well away.

The original path, now much narrower, continues through bracken and across several

If you look down from Coldberry to where the road crosses the beck, then left up the valley, the portal of Pikestone Brow mine can be seen near the beck and close to the remains of a railway box. It is here that our exploration continues. A track branches off the road to the left a short distance from the beck crossing, and leads easily to the mine entrance. Some years ago, when my son was engaged in a school project on lead mining we explored this tunnel. The roof of the first section, perhaps 100 metres long, is supported by cut stone as seen at the entrance. Further in the tunnel passes through the horizontal strata and is self support-

Pikestone Brow mine.

small streams to arrive at, at least in wet weather, a spectacular waterfall. The surprise is that the water comes out of a hole in the rock only fifty centimetres or so square. It is here at Racketgill hush that the path ends.

I am certain that a determined walker with a penchant for bracken and bog could continue exploration until Hudeshope Beck disappears into the marsh at Hudeshope Head. The Ordnance Survey map shows another waterfall half a mile further on. If you go there please send me a picture - this photographer is off to point his lens at other subjects - but is still curious about the missing waterfall.

Waterfall at Racketgill and resurgence.

MIDDLETON TO MICKLETON

Mickleton is the next village downstream from Middleton. Set high above river level and built in several tiers it boasts two pubs, a splendid village hall and a clay pigeon shooting ground among its attractions.

A pleasant half day excursion can be had linking the two communities by way of riverside and field footpaths. Starting in Middleton, walk down Bridge Street and cross the Tees via the County Bridge. A small gate at the end of the bridges gives access to a footpath to Step Ends farm, crosses a small beck and after passing a stand of blackthorn, emerges on to the road near

Looking upstream from County Bridge and a rainbow over Mickleton.

Lonton. Cross the road and take the path to join the old railway line which is followed to Mickleton, traversing the Lunedale viaduct en route.

The railway line continues down the valley but at the picnic site turn left on to the road into Mickleton. Pass through the village hall car park and follow signs

Lunedale Viaduct

to Beckstone Wath Bridge. The bridge was built amid some controversy in 2000. The way lies over the river following the footpath upstream.

The path is good, though muddy in places after rain, but is not level, several gills needing to be negotiated along the way. Much sterling work has been done

Beckstones Wath Bridge.

here; only the provision of causeways, bridges and flights of steps make this walk possible. The following photograph, taken from the road near Whistle Crag, shows an 'aerial' view of the route.

From Whistle Crag

This photograph, taken from river level, is looking back towards Lune Foot where the river Lune enters the Tees. A clear view of the confluence is obscured in high summer because of the density of the foliage on the riverside trees. The final flight of steps leads to a bench dedicated to the memory of Frank Lockwood.

Beyond the bench the path leaves the confines of the river bank and emerges into open country. There is a choice of routes into Middleton from here. To the right the way lies across fields with views of Kirk Carrion and Green Fell while to the left (recommended) the path follows the river past Leekworth Farm to arrive ultimately at the County Bridge. If preferred the river bank can be left earlier at New Town (houses on the right) and the lane followed to Masterman Place and the centre of the village.

Returning to Mickleton, opposite the Blacksmith's

Lune Foot, Stotley and Green Fell.

Arms, a single track road climbs steeply to Bail Hill. The name suggests that iron ore was once extracted and smelted here, but I can find no evidence of this. The top of the hill provides spectacular panoramic views of the upper dale from Kirkcarrion in the west to Eggleston in the east, as well as 'plan' views of Middleton and Mickleton.

Looking west from Bail Hill

Looking towards Eggleston

LUNEDALE AND BALDERSDALE

Two major tributaries of the Tees graced with the title 'river' are the Lune and the Balder. Long Grain and Lune Head Beck join forces at Grains o' the Beck to from the Lune, which within a few hundred metres is captured by Selset reservoir. Selset, opened in 1960, and is used to maintain the level of Grassholme reservoir which, along with Hury in Baldersdale, provides the water supply to much of Teesside.

In the late nineteenth century the burgeoning population of Middlesbrough necessitated the building of reservoirs to supply the demand. Teesdale was chosen

Left, Grains o' the Beck and above, Lunedale and Selset

because of the large catchment area and suitable geological conditions. Hury, started in 1884, was the first to be built. It was followed by Blackton in 1896. Grassholme was started in 1910 and took fourteen years to complete.

No sooner does the Lune escape from Selset - the

Grassholme from Selset Dam

stretch between the first two bridges in the preceding photograph might just be considered river - than it is imprisoned by Grassholme. The lake is stocked with trout by Northumbrian Water and is a popular fishery. It's also a good place to photograph weather!

Below Grassholme the river becomes more secre-tive and flows, for the most part, through a deep wood-ed gorge without much in the way of footpaths. It makes its final public appearance at Lune Bridge just outside Mickleton, before joining the Tees at Lune foot.

Black Beck and Balder Beck unite high on

A stormy evening at Grassholme

Stainmore Common to give birth to the infant River Balder which runs free for about a mile until it suffers a similar fate as the Lune and is impounded, this time by Balderhead reservoir. Balderhead is the most recent of the Baldersdale reservoirs, being built in 1965, and it shows. Further down the valley at Blackton and Hury, built in a more aesthetic era, cut stone, even battlements are in evidence. This is not the case at Balderhead where utility is the word that comes to mind.

The landscape of upper Baldersdale is classified, as is much of the area, as high moorland plateau, and is a product of the last glaciation when the Pennines were scoured by ice sheets. It is characterised by gently rolling, rounded hills covered, for the most part, by a

River Lune, above and the River Balder

River Balder entering Balderhead Reservoir

thick layer of peat and rough vegetation. Only occasionally are the underlying strata of sandstones and millstone grit exposed. There are two such examples in Baldersdale: in the west is Shacklesborough and further east, above Hury, is Goldsborough. Both exhibit steep-sided, rocky, flat-topped summits.

Shacklesborough

It seems, to one who hasn't tried, that the summit of Shacklesborough (right to roam regulations permitting) may be gained by starting at the far end of Balderhead dam on the water side footpath and bearing half left. A clear day will be needed for the expedition as the summit is not in view from the end of the dam.

Miss it and the next link with civilisation is the A66 over Stainmore! By comparison the top of Goldsborough is easily attained. The Pennine Way passes just to the right of it, leaving only a short scramble to the summit.

To be honest the view from the top is not signifi-

Goldsborough

cantly better than that from the road, but it's an interesting place to be. The rock formations, which provide a number of intriguing boulder problems for aspiring

rock climbers, are not typical of the dale where outcrops are predominantly of whin-sill. Here they are of hard sandstone and millstone grit, more usually associated with the southern Pennines.

Before digressing to Shacklesborough and Goldsborough, we left the Balder entering Balderhead reservoir. The dam completed in 1965, was the highest earth embankment dam in England. The maximum water depth is almost 52 metres, giving a capacity of 19.67 million cubic metres of water, collected from a catchment area of twenty square kilometres.

As if this wasn't enough, the next reservoir, Blackton, starts immediately below the dam. On the left bank is Birk Hat Farm, former home of Hannah Hauxwell of *Too Long a Winter* fame. Grassland here, rich in wild flowers, is preserved by the Durham Wildlife Trust as Hannah's Meadow.

Above, Hury from Goldsborough and, right, Blackton and Hury.

Blackton is a little gem of a reservoir. Pleasant water-side paths afford the opportunity to observe a wide variety of bird life, including mistle and song thrush, wheatear, meadow pipit, skylark, herons, curlew and raucous oyster catchers. A bird hide is provided at Birk Hat for those with more than a passing interest in bird watching.

However, all is not sweetness and light. Blackton does not always present the smiling face pictured on the previous page. After heavy rain, water cascades into the overflow shaft producing clouds of spray. It may only be going down to Hury, but under a lowering sky, it looks more like an entrance to the underworld.

Hury was the first reservoir to be built in Teesdale to supply drinking water to Darlington. Pipelines were used to carry the raw water to the Tees Cottage pump-

Overflow at Blackton

ing station and Broken Scar treatment works in the town. This is the last of the Baldersdale reservoirs and, like Blackton, is a haven for bird life, in particular Canada geese and numerous other wildfowl. The lake, now stocked as a trout fishery, is popular, particularly the north shore, with walkers and picnickers.

On its release from Hury, no doubt thinking that it's suffered enough ignominies, the Balder enters a thickly wooded gorge, largely out of sight of prying eyes, for its final couple of miles before joining the Tees at the Hagg in Cotherstone.

Above, rowans at Hury and, to the right, Balder foot, Cotherstone.

MICKLETON TO ROMALDKIRK

To the best of my knowledge there is no riverside path between the villages of Mickleton and Romaldkirk. The path downstream of Beckstones Bridge escapes through Ornella Farm in the direction of Eggleston, leaving views of this section of the river to local landowners and members of Darlington Angling Club. Consequently this chapter will, of necessity, be an eclectic mix of photographs taken in the general area.

Although riverside access is for the most part denied, there is a way of linking the two villages in the shape of the old railway line (a victim of the Beeching axe) between Barnard Castle and Middleton. This, now developed as a walker's highway, and equipped with several benches en route provides easy walking and good views across the valley to the fells above Eggleston.

It's a sobering thought that my first visits to Teesdale were in a train drawn by a steam locomotive along this track. Now mature trees line the way - *tempus fugit* - not half!

The starting point is at the picnic site (where cars can be left) reached by following the lane opposite the

Sunset at Grassholme

Mickleton from Bail Hill

Blacksmith's Arms up the hill for a couple of hundred yards. The car park is on the right. The way ahead is obvious. Views to the right of the track are largely obscured by the slopes of Lund Hill with its plantation of pines, but the vista across the valley, particularly when the fell tops are purple with heather blossom, are well worth the modest effort required. The path arrives at the old railway station, complete with signal post,

Towards Eggleston

just outside Romaldkirk.

The dwellings of the chocolate box village of Romaldkirk, mostly built around 1700, surround the well manicured greens. Officially there are three greens - upper, lower and Monks - but you could make it four depending on what are counted as boundaries. The old pumps which served as the only water supply for the village until well into the 20th century, can still be seen on the upper and lower greens. The stocks, which fell out of use somewhat earlier, remain within crawling distance of the Kirk Inn.

Romaldkirk has a long and chequered history. It is recorded in the Domesday Book in 1086 as being of little worth following its destruction by marauding Scots. Prosperity returned over the next 300 years but unfortunately so did the Scots, who once again wreaked havoc. In common with most of the rest of England, the village was devastated by the Black Death in the mid-17th century with a large part of the population succumbing to the disease.

Opposite the Rose and Crown sits a building constructed in memory of Edward VII. Anywhere else this would be called the village hall but, this being Romaldkirk, it glories in the title of the Reading Rooms! The road bends to the left after the church (more about St. Romald's in the next chapter), and passes Hutchinson Terrace which was originally built in the late 17th century as almshouses to accommodate

Stocks and pumps at Romaldkirk

six of the parish poor, providing they were of suffi-ciently high moral standards. The present building dates from 1829.

The road continues past the cemetery to a T-junc-tion. The left fork leads back to Mickleton passing Hayberries picnic site. This nature reserve on the site of an old sand quarry, looks rather raw at the time of writing but will mature in time.

As stated earlier, there is a lack of footpaths in the immediate area and consequently, if returning to Mickleton, there is no alternative but to follow the road. By way of compensation, the views across the Tees in the direction of Burn Foot beyond Eggleston are good.

Left, Hayberries and above, looking from Hayberries to Burn Foot

ROMALDKIRK TO COTHERSTONE

Romaldkirk is dominated by its church often called the 'Cathedral of the Dales.' Standing on the site of an earlier Saxon church, the present building has its roots in Norman times, but has been considerably extended. The south aisle, chancel and tower were added at roughly one hundred year intervals such that,

by the end of the 15th century, the building would have looked as it does today. Legend has it that St. Romald was baptised at three-days-old, and immediately preached a sermon and promptly died! A pleasant circular walk using field and riverside paths can be taken from here.

At the bottom end of the village a path leads off to the left and very soon crosses Beer Beck. The beck is spanned by a rudimentary foot bridge but this will not be needed except after heavy rain, as adjacent stepping stones are more than adequate. The way continues across the field behind the cemetery bearing slightly right to a stile at the top of a short incline. Wide ranging views of the upper dale are ahead, particularly the fells around Hudeshope above Middleton; the large wood high on the opposite hillside is the Stobgreen plantation on Colley Hill.

A glance over the right shoulder will reveal the route over Barnley which will be taken in due course. A short way further on is a somewhat incongruous breeze-block wall, the only one I can think of anywhere in the dale. At least it provides confirmation, if this was

St. Romald's

required that the correct route is being followed. The path leaves the company of the wall to descend obliquely across the field (good view of Eggleston Hall) and after crossing a stile joins the road a little way above Eggleston Bridge. A short walk along the road to the bridge is unavoidable but it's not far and down hill so can be tolerated. The views of the river both up and downstream from the bridge are good and

Eggleston Hall and Bridge

Wild garlic, bluebells and snowdrops

can be safely appreciated thanks to passing places on both sides. It's sometimes possible to see salmon entering the pool below the bridge but a long wait might be required.

On the other side of the bridge an access road for Northumbria Water leads along the side of the wood. This is a haven for wild flowers, particularly in spring. Snowdrops are the first to arrive, followed by bluebells and primroses. A little later wild garlic adds a pungency all of its own, covering the woodland floor in swathes of white blossom.

The road arrives at a telemetry station controlling the outfall of a tunnel linking the Tees to the River Wear and ultimately Kielder reservoir in Northumberland. Though not a particularly pretty

sight, it only take a few minutes to continue a few yards down the steps to have a look at it. I've lived in the area for over twenty years and only once seen water being discharged into the river.

The path climbs steeply up through the wood to emerge in open fields. The way ahead is obvious and well sign-posted but, a word of caution, if cows with calves are encountered en route, give them a wide berth, particularly if there is a dog in the party and never get between a cow and her calf. Accidents have happened.

The way continues straight ahead past East Barnley farmhouse, which is curiously pebble-dashed, and crosses Raygill Beck. The views become more extensive here; the fells around Baldersdale playing a major

The Kielder tunnel outfall and the River Tees near the tunnel.

role with our old friends Shacklesborough and Goldsborough prominent on the horizon.

The next section provides a prickly problem passing as it does through a stand of gorse bushes before

The view across to Baldersdale

arriving at the edge of a caravan site. Crossing the site is brief and a gate gives access to a track descending the slope. A fork on the right at the bottom of the track leads through more gorse to a footbridge over the Tees.

After crossing the bridge the path turns to the right

and follows the thickly wooded river bank before crossing fields to pass through the yard at Woden Croft. A little further on a stile next to a five-bar gate provides access to a track through more woods. There are a couple of short but steep muddy climbs in this section that require care in wet weather. After about half a mile the path leaves the wood and passes an abandoned farmhouse at Low Garth. The people may have gone but damson trees in the overgrown garden still bear a heavy crop of fruit. From here the way crosses the field to enter a land which emerges close to the Kirk Inn in Romaldkirk.

Gorse on the Hagg, Cotherstone, and Cotherstone Footbridge

COTHERSTONE TO BARNARD CASTLE

Cotherstone is the next village down the valley from Romaldkirk and has a good community feel about it. Built around two greens and the connecting road it boasts church, chapel, two pubs, shop-cum-post office and the local primary school.

A lane opposite the Fox and Hounds leads steeply downhill to an area known as the Hagg where there is parking on hard standing for perhaps half a dozen cars. The remains of Cotherstone castle are close by but little can be seen due to the ravages of the Scots in the 14th century.

A footpath crosses bridges over the Balder and the Tees and follows the Teesdale Way downstream across the field between colourful thickets of gorse to arrive near Cotherstone Crag. A steep ascent through the wood leads, without difficulty or danger, to the top of the crag. The path continues over the fields, passing West Holme and East Holme on the way. There is little to cause excitement here; the Tees retires into its wooded gorge and is largely out of sight but remains within earshot. Notable along the way is an extensive plantation of Scots Pine and an iron fence presumably marking an estate boundary.

About a third of a mile beyond East Holme House an alternative path leads down to the river which it follows through woods to Barnard Castle. The field path skirts the wood and passes close to the eastern abutment of a viaduct which once carried the railway across the Tees. Its location is not obvious in summer being obscured by the dense foliage of trees, but a stand of oaks to the left of the path gives a clue to its position. Although only one arch remains, it is well worth the short detour to view the quality of the masonry and reflect on an age when craftsmanship was not sacrificed on the altar of utility.

After a short distance the path enters Flatts Wood and bends to the right to arrive at the 'Silver Bridge' - technically an aqueduct - over the Tees. The Silver Bridge marks the completion of the outward leg of the

day's excursion. The return trip can be made via paths on the opposite side of the river.

A bridle path leaves the main road on the right after a few yards and leads upstream over land once used by the army as a tank training ground (the curious brick building on the left was used to load up the fighting vehicles), and crosses Scur Beck, passing Tees Cottage before entering Pecknell Wood. A flight of steps climbs the slope to the western abutment of the viaduct from where the old railway line is followed for a short distance before turning off on the road to the right towards Towler Hill Farm.

A footpath leaves the road on the left shortly before it reaches Towler Hill Farm and leads initially across

Barnard Castle silhouette and a winter morning

fields before following the edge of the wood high above the river. Several gills are crossed en route (some provided with bridges) until the path descends through the wood. Look out for primroses here in spring and shooting parties in winter. At the base of the slope the path crosses Grise Beck by means of a footbridge composed of a single stone slab. Here a tree with a swollen lower trunk affords a comfortable seat for several people from which to survey the scene. And a pleasant scene it is, provided one does not look at the attempt at creating a flight pond for duck shooting close to the river. Its design appears to be based on that of an ancient motte castle with moat - a mound of spoil surrounded by a muddy ditch!

From Grise Beck a track (beware Land Rovers)

The Tees from Towler Hill and a bridge over Grise Beck

ascends the hillside passing a log cabin on the left and commences a level section with good views down to the river and the thickly wooded slopes opposite. These are the woods near West Holme passed earlier in the day. The next habitation encountered is Cooper House. There is a choice of routes from here; the lane can be followed directly back into Cotherstone but

doing so will miss out an interesting section of the walk. The better way is to continue past Cooper House - the right of way passes directly behind the house or, more considerately alongside the wall and over a ladder stile, to descend to a bridge across a beck.

After a short distance the path follows a flight of greasy steps up through the wood and arrives unex-

Pastoral scene at Cooper House

pectedly at the base of a line of low cliffs. The rock appears to be sandstone (though I'm no expert) with at least two caves, or are they just big holes? Emerging into the daylight at Mill Hill the walker is greeted with the incongruous sight of a length of motorway crash barrier. Could this be thought an unnecessary intrusion? Not when you look at the drop to the Tees behind

Cliffs near Mill Hill and the path through the wood.

it. More commodiously, a broken wall a few yards further on provides comfortable seating beneath a hawthorn but wearers of short sleeves beware, a mischievous nettle is poised at just the right height to inflict maximum irritation - ladies in skirts should also be careful.

It's not often that a walker on a riverside ramble

comes across a grave at the side of the path, but that is the case here. The grave in question is that of Abraham Hilton, "founder of many local charities" who died in 1902 and "was buried here by his own wish." When you look at the view you can understand why. The path continues (keep right) and descends steps to return to the Hagg.

BARNARD CASTLE TO THE MEETING OF THE WATERS

The Butter Market

Barnard Castle, affectionately known as 'Barney' is the undisputed capital of Teesdale. This bustling market town (market day Wednesday) is well served with shops, pubs and restaurants catering for all tastes. It is the home of the district council and even boasts its own newspaper, the Teesdale Mercury, printed and published here since 1854.

The town is dominated by its castle, built by Bernard Balliol, hence the name, around 1125, on land given to his family following the Norman Conquest. However, its roots go even further back. Galgate, the main street in the upper part of the town follows the line of a Roman road. The castle was a formidable fortress, once owned by Richard III, and defended the settlement until its defenses were breached following a siege in 1569. Its fortunes declined over the ensuing 300 years when it was used as a convenient quarry to provide building stone for various projects including, most notably, Raby Castle, near Staindrop.

Conspicuous in the townscape is the octagonal Butter Market, built by one Thomas Breaks and given to the town in 1747. The building has been put to many uses over the years, including fire station, town hall, court house and gaol. Two bullet holes in the weather vane testify to a competition of marksmanship between a soldier and a gamekeeper in 1804. The shots were fired from the steps of the Raby Arms further up the street.

Barney has had no shortage of illustrious visitors throughout its history. Charles Dickens stayed here at the Kings Head while researching his novel *Nicholas Nickleby* and it is thought that the clock maker at Amen Corner (close to the church) gave him the idea for Master Humphrey's Clock. The artist Turner painted landscapes including the castle and river banks and Sir Walter Scott found inspiration here for his epic poem Rokeby.

Perhaps the most infamous visitor to the town was the Lord Protector of England, Oliver Cromwell, who stayed at what is now Blagraves House (the oldest house in the town) on his way to Richmond in 1648. Fortunately the good people of Barnard Castle were sufficiently puritan for him and he left without causing any harm. John Wesley also used Blagraves at a time when Methodism was frowned on by the established church; evidence of a meeting place was discovered in an attic of the house.

Originally the main centre of population in the town was below The Bank, in the area around Bridgegate. People were attracted by the employment provided by the mill complexes on the riverside. Thorngate Mill, now converted to luxury apartments, produced carpets and Ullathorne's Mill, a little further upstream, made shoe thread. Ullathorne's Mill was demolished in the 1970s after lying in disuse for many years.

Living conditions were by modern standards appalling. Disease was rife, caused by overcrowding and lack of any sanitation or adequate water supply. Waste, both human and animal (livestock was often kept alongside housing) was channelled into surface drains leading to the river. Inevitably the water supply derived from shallow wells became contaminated, leading to an

Blagraves House

epidemic of cholera in 1849 which killed 145 people. It is not surprising that those with the means to do so chose to live away from the stench of the industrial areas and settled in the upper reaches of the town around Galgate and the Market Place.

The most impressive (and incongruous) building by far in Barnard Castle is the Bowes Museum, reached via Newgate from the Butter Market. Modelled on a French chateau it was built by John and Josephine Bowes to house their collection of art and furniture. Unfortunately neither survived to see the project completed; Josephine died in 1874 followed by John in 1885. Opened in 1892, it contains a fine art gallery with paintings by El Greco, Goya and Canaletto among others as well as exhibitions of furniture and porcelain. A particular favourite of visitors is the Silver Swan. This 18th century musical automaton, housed close to the museum entrance, is set in motion several times

daily. Spectators watch as it preens its silver feathers, catches a fish and, without more ado, swallows it whole.

At the bottom of Bridgegate the Tees is spanned by the County Bridge, so called because the Tees marked the boundary between the counties of Durham and North Yorkshire before local government reorganisation. Legend has it that illicit wedding ceremonies were once performed half way across the bridge so as to escape the jurisdiction of both the dioceses of Durham and York.

The bridge was actually built in 1569 and not 1596 as claimed by the date carved into the parapet on the Barnard Castle side of the structure. Occasionally it has to be closed for maintenance or repair. This causes havoc for those living on the southern side of the river who need to commute to the northern side. The

County Bridge and the Demesnes

nearest alternative crossings being, upstream at Eggleston or downstream at Abbey Bridge - both involve a considerable detour.

Anyway, back to following the river. Opposite the Blue Bell at the bottom of the Bank a road leads to an open area called the Demesnes. A footpath from here leads to Abbey Bridge further downstream. Below Barnard Castle the Tees finally quits the deep gorge it

Looking upstream towards Barnard Castle

has occupied since Eggleston and enters a more serene section of its course. For pure sylvan beauty the next mile takes some beating.

The path continues along the riverside past the ruins of Egglestone Abbey, which may be glimpsed through the trees, high up on the opposite bank and, after passing a line of low crags, climbs up to meet the road to Abbey Bridge. To visit the abbey, cross the bridge and

Egglestone Abbey

An Egglestone Abbey portfolio: day room, above, and church, below.

follow Abbey Lane on the right - information boards provide much enlightenment on its history.

Just above Abbey Bridge the Tees, again in turbulent mood, rushes noisily between massive limestone blocks and again, at least for a short while, flows through a narrow rocky gorge. The path to the riverside leaves Abbey Lane at the bridge and zigzags down through the wood to follow the river towards Rokeby.

Not far along the track is a venerable horse chestnut tree which provides an abundant harvest of conkers usually in early October. Although both my children are now grown up and their children are too young to play conkers, I find it impossible to pass by without filling a pocket with the lustrous nuts fallen from the tree. The path stays in the wood, except for a short

The river above Abbey Bridge and Abbey Bridge

foray around a ploughed field, before emerging onto the road close to Rokeby Grange.

The road is followed for a few hundred yards to a bend, a short descent of the grassy bank and a tight squeeze between a rock and a sycamore gives access to the Greta and its confluence with the Tees.

The Meeting of the Waters

Believe it or not this photograph is the view *upstream* on the Greta and no I haven't (at least on this occasion) been guilty of wonky horizon syndrome; the river really does appear to flow uphill before threading its way between scattered blocks of stone to join the Tees.

IN CONCLUSION

The grand plan (if there was one) in writing this book was to chart the course of the Tees from its source at Tees Head to the Meeting of the Waters near Rokeby. This has been achieved by following the river and visiting the valleys of its major tributaries.

Bowlees Beck and Summerhill Force

However, I am conscious that many delectable places have been omitted because they did not fit in neatly with the text. Hopefully the next few pages will go some way to rectify this situation.

A short but delightful walk from Bowlees picnic site near Low Force follows Bowlees Beck upstream to Gibson's Cave and the waterfall of Summerhill Force.

The Middle Side road leaves Middleton and climbs steeply past Middleton House. Ignore turnings to left and right and continue along this high level route to enjoy panoramic views of the upper dale stretching from Kirk Carrion in the east to (on a clear day) Cross Fell in the west.

The path following the south bank of the Tees upstream from Middleton has been described; however, there is also a path on the north side. It does not offer a through route to anywhere, ending as it does on

The upper dale from Stable Edge

the High Force road, but provides a pleasant evening walk, especially in spring, and interesting views across the river.

A winter exploration is also worthwhile; skeletal trees silhouetted against a lowering sky contrast with the white water of the falls and the russets of decaying bracken replace the verdant greens and blossoms so apparent in the springtime scene.

The picnic site at Bowlees is a popular parking place for visitors to Low Force many of whom simply cross the road and two fields to arrive at the falls. An

Riverside path and winter waterfall

interesting alternative is to turn right in front of the former chapel and take the rising track across the fields to the High Force Hotel passing the prosaically named Ash Hill and Dirt Pit on the way. The riverside path can then be followed back to Bowlees.

An avenue of beech trees briefly accompanies the road out of Ettersgill on its journey to the remote sheep pastures around Scar End.

Winter beeches and wild country near Scar End

The little tree crowned hill of Kirk Carrion is tagged on to the end of Green Fell and sits in the angle between Lunedale and Teesdale. It is in fact a tumulus, visible from many places in the dale, and is thought to mark the last resting place of a chieftain called Caryn. An urn containing ashes and fragments of bone were discovered in the early 19th century inside a small chamber made up of four flat stones placed on edge, a

fifth stone served as a roof for the enclosure. Kirk Carrion is reputedly haunted, though whether the ghost is that of Caryn or the man who disturbed him is a matter for conjecture.

And finally, the best (in the opinion of your humble scribe) half dozen places to be.

Descent from Cronkley Fell towards Falcon Clints in August

High Force from a view point among the junipers

Beck Road in autumn

From Bail Hill

Spring meadows

I hope that this book has rekindled memories in the minds of those readers who already knew Teesdale and perhaps inspires them to return and explore areas away from the main tourist routes. To those unfamiliar with the dale I would say that I hope this has served to stimulate an interest and encouraged them to visit this spectacular region of northern England. A final word of advice, Teesdale is beautiful in all seasons, and although the heather moorland is at its best in August and early September, there is no doubt that spring and autumn provide the most colourful scenery. Regarding the weather, if it looks like it will stay dry, take a coat, if it's raining please yourself!

Woods at Low Force on a spring evening

Sunset from Stable Edge